# LIFE CYCLE OF A...

# Butterfly

## Revised and Updated

Angela Royston

**Heinemann Library**
**Chicago, Illinois**

**H** **www.heinemannraintree.com**
Visit our website to find out
more information about
Heinemann-Raintree books.

**To order:**
☎ Phone 888-454-2279
🖥 Visit www.heinemannraintree.com
to browse our catalog and order online.

©2001, 2009 Heinemann Library
an imprint of Capstone Global Library, LLC
Chicago, Illinois

Edited by Adrian Vigliano and Diyan Leake
Designed by Kimberly R. Miracle and Tony Miracle
Original illustrations ©Capstone Global Library Limited
 2001, 2009
Illustrated by Alan Fraser
Picture research by Tracy Cummins and Heather Mauldin
Originated by Chroma Graphics (Overseas) Pte. Ltd.
Printed in China by South China Printing Company Ltd.

13 12 11
10 9 8 7 6 5 4 3

New edition ISBNs:  978 1 4329 2522 2 (hardcover)
                    978 1 4329 2539 0 (paperback)

**The Library of Congress has cataloged the first edition
as follows:**
Life cycle of a butterfly/ by Angela Royston.
    p. cm.
  Includes bibliographical references and index.
        Summary: Introduces the life of a Monarch
butterfly, form its beginning as a tiny egg laid on a milkweed
leaf through its metamorphosis from a caterpillar to an adult
butterfly.
        ISBN 1-57572-697-1 (lib. Bdg.)
        1. Monarch butterfly—Life cycles—Juvenile
literature. [1.    Monarch butterfly. 2. Butterflies.]
        I. Title.
QL561.D3R695 1998
595.78'9—dc21
                    98-10572

**Acknowledgments**
The author and publishers are grateful to the following for
permission to reproduce copyright material: Dembinsky
Photo Association p. 10 (© S. Moody); DRKphoto p. 26 (©
Fritz Poelking); Getty Images pp. 13 (© David De Lossy), 16
(© Altrendo Nature), 21 (© George Lepp); Nature Picture
Library pp. 17 (© Ingo Arndt), 28 bottom left (© Ingo Arndt);
Photolibrary pp. 6 (© Oxford Scientific Films/Breck P. Kent),
7 (© Oxford Scientific Films/J.A.L Cooke), 9 (© Oxford
Scientific Films/Rudie H. Kuiter), 14 (© Oxford Scientific
Films/Rudie H. Kuiter), 15 (© Oxford Scientific Films/Rudie
H. Kuiter), 19 (© Dan Barba), 20 (© Oxford Scientific Films/
Norbert Wu), 23 (© Oxford Scientific Films/Dan Guravich),
24 (© Oxford Scientific Films/J.A.L Cooke), 25 (© Oxford
Scientific Films/J.A.L Cooke), 27 (© Brian Kenney), 28 top
left (© Oxford Scientific Films/J.A.L Cooke), 28 bottom left
(© Oxford Scientific Films/Rudie H. Kuiter), 29 top right
(© Oxford Scientific Films/J.A.L Cooke), 29 bottom (© Oxford
Scientific Films/J.A.L Cooke), Photoshot p. 22 (© NHPA/
Dr Eckart Pott); Shutterstock pp. 4 (© Leighton Photography
and Imaging), 5 (© GJS), 8 (© Lori Skelton), 11 (© sjgh), 12
(© Cathy Keifer), 18 (© Lori Skelton), 28 top right (© Lori
Skelton), 29 top left (© GJS).

Cover photograph reproduced with permission of Minden
Pictures (© Michael Durham).

Every effort has been made to contact copyright holders of
any material reproduced in this book. Any omissions will
be rectified in subsequent printings if notice is given to the
publisher.

We would like to thank Michael Bright for his invaluable help
in the preparation of this book.

# Contents

Some words are shown in bold, **like this**. You can find out what they mean by looking in the glossary.

# What is a Butterfly?

antennae

This is a swallowtail butterfly.

A butterfly is an **insect**. It has six legs, four wings, and two **antennae**. Many butterflies have brightly colored wings.

| 1 day | 1 week | 4 weeks | 6 weeks |

Monarch butterflies also live in some parts of Europe and Australia.

Many kinds of butterflies live in different parts of the world. The butterfly in this book is a monarch butterfly from North America.

10 weeks

32 weeks

32 weeks

# Butterfly Eggs

This photo is enlarged so the eggs look much bigger than they really are.

Every butterfly begins life as an egg the size of a pinhead. The monarch butterfly lays her eggs on a **milkweed** leaf.

1 day

1 week

4 weeks

6 weeks

Butterfly caterpillars are also called larvae.

Just over a week later, the eggs begin to **hatch**. A small **caterpillar** crawls out of an egg! It ate a hole in the egg, and now it will eat the eggshell.

# A Few Days Later

A fully grown monarch caterpillar is about the size of your thumb.

The **caterpillar** eats and grows bigger. It chews through a **milkweed** leaf with its strong **jaws**. Soon it has eaten a big hole in the leaf.

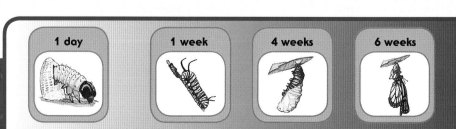

Caterpillars chew using sharp, teethlike points.

All the eggs have **hatched** and many monarch caterpillars are feeding on the milkweed plant. They crawl from leaf to leaf, eating as they go.

10 weeks

32 weeks

32 weeks

# 1 Week

old skin

The old skin is stuck to the stem as the caterpillar pulls itself out.

The **caterpillar** is growing, but its skin is not. One day its skin is so tight it splits open. The caterpillar has a new and bigger skin underneath.

1 day

1 week

4 weeks

6 weeks

The stems on this milkweed plant are covered with hairs.

The caterpillar will shed its skin four times as it grows. It crawls away, clinging to the **milkweed** plant with its many legs.

# 2 Weeks

Most milkweed flowers are pink or pink and white.

The **caterpillar** eats and grows. Other animals do not eat it. **Milkweed** leaves have something in them that makes the caterpillar taste bad.

| 1 day | 1 week | 4 weeks | 6 weeks |
| --- | --- | --- | --- |
|  |  |  |  |

This bird catches insects to feed its young.

Many birds catch **insects**, but they leave the monarch caterpillar alone. They have learned that it tastes bad.

10 weeks

32 weeks

32 weeks

# 4 Weeks

The **caterpillar** is fully grown. It makes a silky pad on a leaf and grasps it. The caterpillar's stripy skin splits for the last time.

Caterpillars hang from the leaf when their skin splits for the last time.

| 1 day | 1 week | 4 weeks | 6 weeks |
|---|---|---|---|
|  |  |  |  |

Underneath the skin is a green **pupa**. The caterpillar is getting ready to change into a butterfly!

A pupa is also called a chrysalis.

# 6 Weeks

The **pupa** takes a few hours to get hard and dry. Inside the hard shell of the pupa, the **caterpillar**'s body changes.

The butterfly grows in the pupa for 10 to 14 days.

| 1 day | 1 week | 4 weeks | 6 weeks |
|-------|--------|---------|---------|

Then the pupa cracks open and the butterfly pulls itself free. At first the butterfly's wings are damp and crumpled. As the wings dry, they slowly open.

When the wings are dry, the butterfly is ready to fly away.

# 8 Weeks

Monarch butterflies have no teeth. They can only suck their food.

tongue

The butterfly flies from flower to flower. It unrolls its long tongue and sucks up the sweet **nectar** in the flowers.

| 1 day | 1 week | 4 weeks | 6 weeks |

Monarch butterflies drink the nectar of many kinds of flowers.

Birds do not try to catch the butterfly. It still has the bad taste that the **caterpillar** had.

10 weeks

32 weeks

32 weeks

# 10 Weeks

It is fall. Short days and colder weather let monarch butterflies know it is time to go to a warmer place.

The monarch butterflies gather together on the branches of trees.

1 day

1 week

4 weeks

6 weeks

Monarch butterflies in the west of North America fly to southern California.

Suddenly they all flutter up into the sky. They fly south until they reach the mountains of Mexico. The weather there is warm even in winter.

10 weeks

32 weeks

32 weeks

# 14–30 Weeks

Gathering together helps monarchs keep warm.

The butterflies are very tired when they get to Mexico. They gather on a pine tree to rest.

1 day | 1 week | 4 weeks | 6 weeks

Some monarchs fly nearly 200 miles a day.

When spring comes, the Sun warms the butterflies. They feed from flowers. Most of the butterflies start to fly north.

10 weeks

32 weeks

32 weeks

# 32 Weeks

This male butterfly has found a female that is ready to mate.

The butterflies rest during the journey. The male butterflies find females that are ready to **mate**. After mating, the females lay their eggs.

| 1 day | 1 week | 4 weeks | 6 weeks |
|---|---|---|---|
|  |  |  |  |

eggs

Females lay their eggs on the undersides of milkweed leaves.

They lay them on **milkweed** plants. The butterflies live only for a few more weeks.

10 weeks

32 weeks

32 weeks

# The Journey Continues

Snow and storms can kill monarchs.

Back in Mexico, some butterflies have been battered by a big storm. Some recover and will fly north. Others will die on the journey.

| 1 day | 1 week | 4 weeks | 6 weeks |
| --- | --- | --- | --- |
|  |  |  |  |

The eggshell is the caterpillar's first meal.

Along the way, **caterpillars** are **hatching**. When they change into butterflies, they will fly north. There they will **mate** and lay eggs of their own.

10 weeks

32 weeks

32 weeks

# Life Cycle

Egg hatching

1 week

4 weeks

6 weeks

10 weeks

32 weeks

32 weeks

# Fact File

- The wings of a monarch butterfly are about 4 inches (10 centimeters) across. This is nearly as wide as your hand span.

- Monarchs fly farther than any other kind of butterfly. During their long journeys north and south they fly up to 1,865 miles (3,000 kilometers).

- Butterflies use their **antennae** to smell and to feel. They smell food and the special chemicals a male monarch gives off when he is trying to **mate**.

- In one day, a **caterpillar** may eat many times its own weight in **milkweed** leaves.

# Glossary

**antennae**  feelers on an insect's head

**caterpillar**  young butterfly or moth before it changes into a pupa

**hatch**  break an egg so that a young caterpillar can come out of it

**insect**  very small animal that has six legs, four wings, and three parts to its body

**jaws**  moving parts of a caterpillar's mouth

**mate**  come together (a male and a female) to produce young

**milkweed**  plant that monarch caterpillars like to eat

**nectar**  sweet juice in some flowers

**pupa**  stage in life when a caterpillar changes into a butterfly or moth

# More Books to Read

Ganeri, Anita. *How Living Things Grow: From Caterpillar to Butterfly*. Chicago: Heinemann Library, 2007.

Theodorou, Rod. *Animal Young: Insects*. Chicago: Heinemann Library, 2007.

# Index